Beattitudes
of MARRIAGE

BY MARK GUNGOR

illustrations by Cara Petrus

TABLE OF CONTENTS

To my darling, Debbie.

NICE

The vast majority of marriages could be greatly improved
if couples would follow this simple advice: **BE NICE.**

BE NICE

THE VAST MAJORITY OF MARRIAGES COULD BE GREATLY IMPROVED IF COUPLES WOULD FOLLOW THIS SIMPLE ADVICE: BE NICE. Oddly enough, many people believe that because they are married, they do not have to be nice. It is as if they think that their marriage license is a license to be mean and nasty. Oh, they would never say that, but that is certainly how they act.

Some of the nicest people in the world – people who would not hurt a fly, those who would brake and swerve for squirrels in the road, guys who would help an old lady cross the road, women who would be thankful and considerate to the pimply-faced kid that bags their groceries, couples who sit together in church smiling, singing and gently nodding their heads to the encouragement of the pastor—these same sweet people…get them home and watch the fireworks as they bark, yell, and throw insults at each other. Again, it is as if they believe a marriage license grants them permission to be however mean they deem necessary; to be as short and impatient as the moment calls for. They think that somehow a marriage license allows them not to live out their Christian faith. "I don't have to be nice—I'm married!!"

Much of this is rooted in the six most poisonous words of bad advice ever given to a generation of married couples: BE HONEST WITH HOW YOU FEEL. Of all the ignorant, moronic and misguided pieces of advice ever given to couples, this ranks right at the top. *Be honest with how you feel.* Good grief!! No wonder they feel they have the right—no, the moral imperative—to emotionally vomit all over each other. They have been deceived into thinking that, not only do they have the right to spew their venom, but that somehow this is good for their marriage. No wonder so many people end up in divorce…

Look, your mama was right: If you don't have something good to say, DON'T SAY IT!!

My wife and I have been married for over 40 years. People always ask, "How have you been married for so long?" My answer: Because we are NOT honest with HOW WE FEEL!!

"Be honest with how you feel." Uuuuugh. Of all the stupid, ignorant and destructive pieces of advice that some idiot with a PhD came up with. Oh, I know, I know…there are times you need to share things that are uncomfortable and there are issues you need to visit and even fight through as a couple, but that it not what I am talking about here. I'm talking about people who just act as if it is their God-given right to be as mean and insulting as they please—just because they are married!

Only in marriage are we so incomprehensibly and immeasurably stupid. In no other area of life would you apply such foolishness. Can you imagine people deciding tomorrow morning on whether or not to go to work based on how they feel? Calling their boss and saying, "Look boss, I'd really love to come to work today, I really would. But I have to be honest with how I feel, and quite frankly…I'm not feeling it. And while we are at it, I feel I really must share that I feel you are an idiot." They'd get fired.

Can you imagine soldiers at the front line when the sergeant yells "Charge!" and one of the soldiers stands up and says, "Um…look guys…I really would love to charge with you, I really would… Many of you know I have been very pro-charging for some time now and have been one of the better chargers during drills. But…I don't feel it would be fair to you if I charged at this time, because…well…quite frankly, I'm not feeling it." They'd take a gun out and shoot him in the head.

Truth is, your ability to succeed in life will be in direct proportion to how little you listen to your feelings. Ever feel like studying? Ever feel like working 18-hour days? Ever feel like practicing piano scales for eight hours a day? Truly successful people do NOT listen to how they feel. Great academics study, successful business people put in whatever hours are necessary, and the greatest concert pianists practice until their minds grow numb. You know who does listen to their feelings? The people who drop out of school, stop when work gets too hard and those who quit taking piano lessons because they feel like they would rather go out and play with their friends. Listening to your feelings is the ultimate separation in life between winners and losers. Those who listen to their feelings fail, and those who don't succeed—period. And the same is true for couples who stay married and those who end up in divorce.

For the love of God—just BE NICE! It is the ultimate guide to all your relational dilemmas.

"Do I have to visit my irritating in-laws?" Yes, be nice.

"What if my wife is grumpy?" Be nice.

"Don't I have the right to criticize my husband when he doesn't fold the clothes the way I told him to?" No, be nice.

"Do I have to help my wife around the house even when I come home tired?" Yes, be nice.

"What do I do if my mother-in-law insults me?" Be nice.

"What if my husband always forgets to take out the garbage, leaves the toilet lid up or fails to pick up his underwear that he left in the middle of the living room just before diner guests arrive!?!" Check your medication and just BE NICE!!

Marriage is hard, but it is not complicated. Want to have a meaningful and successful marriage that will last the rest of your life? Two words: Be Nice.

CONTENT

"I have learned in whatever situation I am to be content. I know how to be brought low, and I know how to abound. In any and every circumstance, I have learned the secret of facing plenty and hunger, abundance and need. I can do all things through him who strengthens me." —Philippians 4: 11-13

BE CONTENT

"I have learned in whatever situation I am to be content. I know how to be brought low, and I know how to abound. In any and every circumstance, I have learned the secret of facing plenty and hunger, abundance and need. I can do all things through him who strengthens me." –Philippians 4: 11-13

TOO MANY PEOPLE LIVE IN THE WORLD OF "I'D RATHER BE…" They'd rather be somewhere else, with someone else, doing something else, looking at something else, listening to something else or feeling something else. They justify their misery by pointing out their lousy circumstances. "If only things would change," then they'd be happy. They have bought into the lie that "the grass is always greener on the other side." Of course, the truth is that the grass is just as crappy over there as it is where you are. Unfortunately, if you believe you cannot be happy because of your circumstances, then you will always be a victim in life.

I often wonder what some Christians are going to do on Judgment Day when they stand with saints of old who suffered the loss of all things, witnessed their children being slaughtered before their eyes, some who had been ripped to pieces by wild animals, refusing to renounce their faith—all the while being filled with an unspeakable joy and full of glory. Then these modern Christians are going to have to explain to God why *they* could not be happy because their husbands did not pick up their underwear or their wives did not give them the level of respect they believe they so richly deserved. *Really?!?*

Being filled with contentment and happiness is a *choice*—it is not the result of everything being just the way you want. Paul wrote to the Philippian church and told them that he had learned the secret to happiness. Have you learned the secret? Did you even know there was a secret?? (Probably not or it wouldn't be a secret.) What was his secret??? To be content, no matter WHAT the circumstances. If he was hungry, he was happy. If he was full, he was happy. If he had lots, he was happy. If he had nothing, he was happy. He had learned the secret: To be content no matter what was going on around him. That is when he said, "I can do all things through him who strengthens me." Many Christians believe that verse is a promise that they can change their circumstances, but it is not. It is a statement that proclaims that we can succeed, be happy and content even if our circumstances NEVER CHANGE!

And seriously?!? You can NOT be happy because your husband doesn't meet your emotional needs? You can NOT be happy because your wife incessantly nags at you? Jesus died on the cross for your sins, empowered you with his Holy Spirit, crowned you with incredible truths and has promised to someday raise you from the dead and give you eternal life, but you STILL cannot be happy?!?

Happiness is a choice, a determination, a commitment.

Yes, you can be happy even if your husband is an intolerable ass. Yes, you can be happy even if your wife is the first cousin of the Wicked Witch of the West. Yes, you can be happy even though it seems your children are demon possessed. Yes, you can be happy even if you don't have enough money. Yes, you can be happy even if your health has turned for the worst. Yes, you CAN be happy…if you can learn the secret: No matter what your circumstances, be content.

Be
CONNECTED

One of the worst things a couple can do is live on their own little island. People who think of their marriage in terms of an isolationist mindset, do so at their own peril.

BE CONNECTED

ONE OF THE WORST THINGS A COUPLE CAN DO IS LIVE ON THEIR OWN LITTLE ISLAND. People who think of their marriage in terms of an isolationist mindset, do so at their own peril. "This is OUR business. No one should know OUR business. Don't tell anyone OUR business." This is the kind of foolish thinking that millions of couples employ today. But I warn you: If you live on your own little island, you will eventually turn into cannibals and start eating each other.

Want to know how you can have a healthy marriage that will last a lifetime? GET A LIFE!! Or more to our point here: GET SOME FRIENDS!!

"But pastor, we DO have friends. I have my friends and he has his friends."

That, my dear, is your problem. Each of you having your own set of friends, surrounding yourself with people who will most likely validate your own self-centered, delusional, selfish viewpoint, is not helpful. Let's face it—

the reason they are your friends is because they think as goofy as you do. It's like Saddam Hussein, during the Gulf War, who surrounded himself with generals who assured him, "Yes your majesty! We have the Americans on the run! You were right, they are suffering from the mother of all battles!!"

When you and your spouse argue, chances are you are more caught up in the *argument* than the actual facts you're debating. Emotions go crazy and you even start to use phrases like, "You ALWAYS do that!" or "You're just like your father!!"

Want to save yourselves thousands of dollars in marriage counseling? Want to avoid the need for professional counseling in the first place? GET SOME FRIENDS!! I mean get other couples that you routinely get together with to talk out the crap in your lives. Nothing is more enlightening than to take one of your stupid fights to your friends and have them tell you, "Boy, that is really stupid."

"I want the thermostat set at 70 and she wants it at 68!!"

You will most likely hear your friends suggest, "Why don't you just set it at 69??"

Ahhh… a brilliant insight. One that should have been obvious to you in the first place, except for the fact that you are mad and only interested in winning. In a phrase: You are too close to the trees to see the forest. Get some friends that can help you with your struggles and you can help them with theirs.

Of course, truly misbehaving individuals will oppose such a scenario at all costs!! Why? Because it is easy to argue their absurd position with their spouse, but they know anyone else would tell them they are wrong.

Your husband thinks it's okay that he looks at porn and has lunch with other women? Try floating that past your couple-friends. They will likely beat him with sticks.

Your wife thinks it's okay for her to travel with other men for work—just the two of them…alone…in hotels? Yeah…try sliding *that* past your friend network.

You see, oftentimes the reason couples do NOT want anyone to know their business is because deep down they know that their "business" is illegal or illegitimate.

Want a happy, healthy, life-long marriage? Get some friends.

Be connected.

Be
PREPARED

Let's face it...LIFE CAN REALLY SUCK.

BE PREPARED

L ET'S FACE IT…LIFE CAN REALLY SUCK.

Oh, our Lord put it a bit more eloquently when he said, *"In this world you will have trouble…"* (John 16:33). But like it or not, at some point, despite your best efforts, eventually…the caca is going to hit the fan.

I am always stunned by people who are "shocked" when things don't go according to plan. Really? So you thought you would just skate through life and nothing would ever go wrong?? Exactly what planet are you on? Even the Apostle Peter had to slap the Christians of his day by asking them, "Why are you surprised that the caca is hitting the fan??!!" Well, that is my translation. What he literally said was, *"Dear friends, do not be surprised at the fiery ordeal that has come on you to test you, as though something strange were happening to you"* (1 Peter 4:12).

Be prepared. Caca happens!! Don't just wander aimlessly through life and then fall apart when unexpected bad things happen.

Here is a bit of a sports analogy… I have never gotten hurt playing football. Basketball, on the other hand, has inflicted me with too many "slings and arrows of outrageous fortune" (William Shakespeare quote. Impressed??) to be numbered. To this day, you will not get me on a court to play basketball.

What is the difference? In football, you anticipate the hit. You are prepared. In basketball, a supposedly "non-contact" sport, you are blindsided constantly. Better to see the tackler coming than to get a ball smacked upside your head when you are not looking.

Be prepared. Anticipate. Brace yourself! Life if full of unanticipated caca.

The following story is true.

The alarm went off at 6:45. I had just flown back from doing one of my Laugh Your Way to a Better Marriage seminars the evening before and struggled to wake up as I needed to get ready to preach four times at our church in Green Bay that Sunday morning.

I looked over at my wife, Debbie, to see how she was doing. She had just started doing chemotherapy to treat the breast cancer they had recently discovered and she was not tolerating it well. They would give her one drug after another to counter the negative affects of some other drug. She found it difficult to sleep at night, but seemed to be resting nicely as I climbed out of bed. I grabbed some appropriate reading materials as I made my way back into the bathroom for my morning "meditations". I closed the door as I entered the bathroom and then closed the second door to the "reflective" room.

Down the stairs in the basement was where one of my younger brothers was staying. He had moved in with us after his wife kicked him out of their home.   He needed a place to stay while he was sorting things out. Our family is of Latino descent and Latinos rarely go homeless—we just move in with a relative. Fortunately for most of us, there always seems to be several to choose from. Being the closest and most available, he moved in with us. We called him our basement troll.

Understandably, his state of affairs was having a very negative effect on his psyche. He was falling further and further into a deep depression. I had yelled at him the night before that he needed to snap out of it. (Apparently, yelling at the depressed is not particularly helpful—who knew??) Unbeknownst to us, he had gone days without sleeping and was on the verge of a manic episode. That morning he snapped and became delusional. He walked up the stairs and started engaging in a heated conversation with me in the kitchen. Only problem: I wasn't in the kitchen—I was still "meditating".

My wife woke up and heard my brother in the kitchen threatening to shoot me. She thought it was unusual that I was not talking back since I am famous for having an opinion about most everything (whether or not I know what I'm talking about never seems to hinder me), and she concluded that I must be frozen in fear. She quickly grabbed her phone and called 911.

"My husband is trapped in the kitchen and his brother is threatening to shoot him!"

"Alright ma'am, the police are on their way."

As my wife stayed huddled in our bedroom, unsure of what would happen next, I walked out of the bathroom wearing nothing but a t-shirt and a smile.

"What are you doing here?!" she whisper loudly. (Apparently, wives can still yell at you even while they are whispering. Again, who knew??)

"Well...I live here."

"I thought you were in the kitchen with your brother!! He was threatening to shoot you! The police just arrived and want us to come out with our hands up!!!"

I thought to myself, "Oh no, the drugs have caused her to go crazy!!" I stared at her in disbelief.

"We need to go outside!!" she stressed.

"I'm naked."

"For heavens sake, get dressed!!!!" Again, the whispering was rather intense.

By now my brother had gone back into the basement, so when I came out of the bedroom, having properly girded my loins of course, there was no brother. I truly thought my wife was losing it. I looked outside and sure enough, there stood a couple of Green Bay's finest, guns at the ready, waving at us to quickly run to them.

"Oh good grief!" I thought to myself. I still thought my wife was imagining the entire conversation as a result of her drugged up state.

We quickly ran over to the officers and my wife repeated what she had heard. After hearing her story, the officer looked at me. I paused. I looked at my wife. I paused. I looked at the police. I paused. I looked back at her.

"Look, my wife is going through chemo and taking all kinds of drugs and she may be hallucinating..." I continued as I tried to explain to the police why we were in this ridiculous scenario.

Now, you should see the kind of look your wife gives you while you are explaining to the police that she is likely not in her right mind. Strangely enough, it is much louder than even the whisper yelling. But what was I to do. There was no brother in the kitchen. I was clearly not in conversation with him. I never heard anything. She was taking a lot of drugs. What would *you* think??

Just then, several squad cars zoomed in, one after another, lining our quiet neighborhood with pretty blinking lights. I watched in horror as officers quickly surrounded our house, their guns pulled and ready. One of the officers yelled over, "He just called in to the police and said he had the house rigged for explosives and was going to blow it up!!" Apparently, our basement troll had indeed completely lost it and was now calling emergency numbers to threaten everyone he could.

I snapped my head over to look at my wife to witness her eyes piercing through my soul as she growled, "I told you so…"

My mind wanted to ponder all the ways my wife would kill me later for telling the police that she was a nut case, but instead I had this horrifying thought: WHAT WOULD THE NEIGHBORS THINK???!!!! All they had to do is look out their windows and witness the local pastor's house surrounded by police, guns at the ready, and the road covered with cars that were blinking red and blue. I could imagine my elderly neighbor saying to his wife, "I knew that man was unstable. They're probably operating a crack house over there…"

My thoughts were broken as a police officer looked me squarely in the face and with all sincerity asked of me, "Sir, do you have any explosives in the house?!"

"What??!!" I retorted. "Who has explosives in their house????!!!!"

"Sir, he has threatened to blow the house up."

"Oh for heavens sake," having finally gotten a sense of just what was going on, "it's just my brother in the basement. Clearly he has had a mental lapse due to his depression. Just go down there and get him!"

As the police were discussing the best and safest way to apprehend a basement troll, I soon found myself texting my staff that I just might be a little late for the service. You would think they would have been greatly surprised to hear that I was stuck at home, surrounded by a S.W.A.T team. Oddly enough they simply responded, "No problem". Apparently, they have become comfortable with the unexpected when it comes to their pastor.

Finally, with the troll in handcuffs, the police put my brother in a squad car and took him off to the local mental health facility. I was relieved that my home no longer had the appearance of a crack house under siege, and happy that the police cars had cleared the neighborhood.

After getting dressed and kissing my wife (who was still slightly irritated that I tried to tell the police she was a nut case), I drove to church to preach the first of four sermons.

What did we do after it was all over? We laughed. We laughed really, really, hard. Oh, I know, there should have been a degree of compassion for my poor brother (by the way, a few days of R&R at our local mental health retreat center and he was much better). There probably should have been a sense of embarrassment for the display we put on for our neighbors, but they probably think we're crazy already. And, of course, there should have been some remorse for the rambling sermons I had just preached, though my loving congregation was very understanding.

No, we weather such storms on a regular basis with good humor. Why? Because we expect the storms to come. When? *Not sure.* How intense? *Unknown.* But we are never shocked when they arrive.

I already told you that Jesus said, "In this world you will have trouble." But he went on to say, "Be of good cheer. I have overcome the world."

Be prepared.

Be
PROACTIVE

"Do not be deceived: God cannot be mocked.
A man reaps what he sows." – Galatians 6:7

BE PROACTIVE

"Do not be deceived: God cannot be mocked. A man

reaps what he sows." — Galatians 6:7

HERE IS A TRUTH THAT MANY DO NOT WISH TO ACKNOWLEDGE: YOU REAP WHAT YOU SOW. Do you have a sucky marriage? It's because you are doing sucky things—period. Oh, I know, I know… it's not your fault; it's the other person. It's not fair, you married Satan's cousin (though, admittedly, twice removed…), you married the wrong person, you married too soon, too young, too fat, too tall, he votes Democrat (well, that might explain a few things…), she's too needy, it's the in-laws, it's the kids, we're too busy, it rained last week, the cat ate the hamster…on and on it goes. But no matter how hard you run from it, God will *not* be mocked; you will reap what you sow.

Now, in all fairness, you may not know what to sow (do) in your marriage to get the results you desire. That is why you purchased this book and why you should purchase every book I write, DVD I release, read every blog I post and tune into every TV/Radio show I broadcast. (*This shameless plug was brought to you by Laugh Your Way America! LLC.*) Trying to learn and gain insights is always a good thing. The Bible tells us to seek out wisdom above all else. Just always be careful to remember: You reap what you sow. And at some point you have to not just learn, but DO.

I am stunned how few people see the connection between what they do and what they get in life. There are people who believe they should have as much money as the next person, even though they don't work for it or save. Students want a passing grade in school even though they never studied. Work for welfare benefits? Outrageous!! Millions of people today want equality of outcomes—not just equality of opportunities. They think they should get all the benefits of life, well… just because. This is true of many people's approach to marriage. They think they should be happy, well…just because!

"Pastor, our marriage is terrible. We have no connection and seem to be continually drifting further apart. Why is that?"

"Do you ever spend time with each other?"

"Well, we are kind of busy."

"Do you talk at the end of the day?"

"Well, we are pretty tired and we really want to watch the LATE SHOW before we go to bed."

"Do you guys ever have a date night with just the two of you and no kids?"

"No, we think that is unfair to the kids."

"Do you do ANYTHING together?"

"Not really. So…why do you think we are struggling?"

SERIOUSLY!?! Suggest to these clueless souls that the reason their marriage is so lacking is because they don't put any effort into it and they stare at you with a hollow glaze.

It's like the people who never pray, attend church only twice a year, haven't turned a page in their Bibles in three years and they ask, "Why does God seem so far away??"

Like the guy who never makes any effort at work and wonders why he always gets passed over for promotion.

Like the woman who criticizes everyone she knows and then wonders why she doesn't have any friends.

Like the guy who always drives too fast and complains about all the speeding tickets he gets.

Like the guy who yells and curses at his wife and wonders why he doesn't get any sex.

Like the woman who always disrespects and belittles her husband and then wonders why he isn't passionate about her.

The analogies go on and on and on. And sadly, most of us know people like this. People seem to have lost the connection between what they do and what they get.

Well, whether they get the connection or not, the rule never changes and it doesn't matter how much you desire a different outcome: You will reap what you sow.

Be proactive.

Be

CLEAR

There are few things as frustrating in a marriage than
when one person thinks they are being clear
—but in fact, **THEY ARE NOT**.

BE CLEAR

THERE ARE FEW THINGS AS FRUSTRATING IN A MARRIAGE THAN WHEN ONE PERSON *THINKS* THEY ARE BEING CLEAR—BUT IN FACT, THEY ARE NOT.

This is particularly the case with the more "emotive" spouse. I say spouse because, despite the stereotype, it can often be the man instead of the woman. It is not that the emotive one seeks to be troublesome. It is just that the emotive spouse feels soooo deeply about everything, they just cannot comprehend that the other person could be so void of the obvious.

"Why are you upset?"

"You know why I am upset!"

"No, I don't."

"I clearly communicated that you really hurt me when you failed to do what I needed you to do."

"You did?"

"Yes!!"

"When did you do that?!"

"Remember in the middle of all that work in the kitchen when we were so busy?"

"Ummmm…yeah…"

"Well, don't you remember when I sighed really long?"

"I guess so."

"Well, that was my way of telling you I was really, really upset!"

"What?!? I just thought you had gas."

"You are so insensitive!!"

You see, emotive people think they are clearly communicating when they sigh, blink, gaze, shrug, frown, scratch, belch or sulk. They are so in touch with their own emotions, they think it is impossible for the other person not to interpret their signals. But they can't interpret. Truth be told, the only person who could even begin to pick up on their "secret signals" is another totally emotive person. (Someone, by the way, whom they usually confide in that totally validates their signals, completing their self-delusion that they were, in fact, being clear.) But to the non-emotive person, a grunt is a grunt, a sigh is just a sigh, and a strange look on your face is probably just an indication that you are breaking wind. To them, it is *not* a revealing of your soul and certainly not a clarification of the state of your soul. If you want them to know what and how you are feeling, you actually have to tell them.

This is unwelcomed news for the emotive ones, but it doesn't change the fact: Your spouse doesn't know what you want because you don't *tell* them—period.

SPOT QUIZ: How can you tell who is the more emotive one in the marriage?

ANSWER: Look at whoever is usually upset.

Do you want something? ASK for it.

Are you feeling something? SAY it. (But remember Chapter 1 and BE NICE!)

Are you in need of something? TELL them what it is.

In short: BE CLEAR.

Don't go about in your delusional non-sense state of, "If they really cared about me, they would know how I'm feeling!" No, no, no, no, no!! Truth be told, your emotive whining can be so taxing, so exhausting, so irritating, so boring and so bothersome that the other person actually STOPS trying to understand you. They get tired of being wrong in their interpretation of your mystical signals and at some point they just quit trying.

Oh, I know, I know…your non-emotive spouse is insensitive, uncaring, unfeeling, and (due to their genealogical lineage to Satan himself) just evil!! Yeah, yeah, yeah…blah, blah, blah.

Here's a suggestion: How about you break out of your narcissistic, self-centered orbit, and instead of complaining about what your spouse doesn't naturally understand about you, *just tell them.*

Be clear.

DOERS

"Be doers of the word, and not hearers only, deceiving yourselves." –James 1:22

BE DOERS

"Be doers of the word, and not hearers only, deceiving yourselves." – James 1:22

I AM ALWAYS STUNNED TO SEE HOW MANY PEOPLE FAIL TO LIVE OUT THEIR FAITH AT HOME. When they are at work or play or church they seem conscious to be a good witness of their Christian faith: Being kind to the unkind, loving to the unlovely, patient with the impatient, helping the weak, feeding the poor or clothing the naked. They sing, they smile, they are a wonderful reflection of the face of God in a lost world. They give, they share, they bless…until they get home!! Then, it seems, the kind Dr. Jekyll turns into the frightening Mr. Hyde. All the love, kindness and patience they exhibit to the world suddenly disappears once they get behind the closed doors of home.

Maybe you've been there. Yelling and biting at each other's heels as you get ready for church, sniping at each other while driving in the car, fuming as you walk through the parking lot, and then suddenly, as you walk through the doors of the church, an amazing transformation takes place!! The smile that comes on your face, the gentle tone in which you speak, the loving way you embrace others. Ahhhh…it is so sweet, so wonderful, so "godly". Some would call it a minor miracle. Most of us, however, call it being a hypocrite.

I know we hate to admit it, but the truth is, we are only as spiritual as we are when we are at home. The Apostle John said that if we cannot love our brother that we can see, we cannot love God whom we cannot see—and I'm pretty sure that applies to our spouse as well.

Look, I don't care how sweet you present yourself to the world. If you can't live your faith at home—you can't live it, period. I know it can be a bit disturbing to admit, but your relationship with your spouse is a direct reflection of your true spirituality. Not good news for the many pastors and ministers who divorce their spouses. Oh, they claim to really love Jesus—they just can't seem to stay married. Really??

We need to be actual DOERS of the word. And that starts at home.

Here is an observation of the difference between the sexes—and I know, I know, these are big generalities, but they are generally true: When a man hears the truth, he feels compelled to act upon the truth. Of course, most men fight this by simply not listening. In fact, I dare say that when it comes to matters of truth, a great many men respond by saying, "I don't want to hear it!!" If I had a dollar for every time a man yelled, *"I don't want to hear it!"* I would be a very wealthy man.

Women, on the other hand, due to their love of words, rejoice in hearing the truth! Their problem is this: They don't actually want to *do* it. In fact, many of them delay *doing* the right thing by asking a million questions about what is the right thing to do.

If I have a hundred men sitting in a room and I quote to them from Ephesians 5 and say, "You men need to love your wives like Christ loved the church," there would be an immediate sense for them to act on what they just heard. Oh, they may regret hearing it, but make no mistake: They know the truth when they hear it and feel compelled to act on it (not that they always do, but they will feel it).

Now, if I have a hundred women sitting in a room and I quote to them from Ephesians 5 and say, "You women need to respect your husbands," you know what I would get?

"What do you mean by respect?"

"Do you have a book about respect?"

"Can we do a women's Bible study on respect?"

"Please preach a sermon series on respect."

You see, they love to hear—just not so crazy about doing. But asking lots of questions about the truth does not give you permission not to act on the truth.

Guys, you need to listen. Ladies, stop with the 15 million versions of "Why is that?"

Be doers.

PATIENT

Building a life together takes time.
It just doesn't happen **OVERNIGHT**.

BE PATIENT

BUILDING A LIFE TOGETHER TAKES TIME. IT JUST DOESN'T HAPPEN OVERNIGHT. Oftentimes, the journey to reach your dreams can take decades. Oh sure, some get there rather quickly, but for most of us, getting the life we dream of takes a really, really, really long time.

Too many young people, as soon as they graduate from high school or college, look at what their parents have and just assume they will have that level of comfort and success as soon as they launch out on their own. What they fail to realize is that it took their parents decades to get to that point and it will most likely take them the same amount of time, if not longer. While the Bible says that when a man and wife join together the *two shall become one*, the reference is actually about the sexual union. In that sense they become "one" right away. But to truly become one unit that functions with one direction and one purpose…well, that takes time. Sometimes a really long time.

Be patient. Even if things seem like they are so terrible you cannot possibly stand another moment—be patient. Things change.

A study from the University of Chicago looked at couples who were married and miserable (I call them M&Ms). Half of the miserable couples, in an attempt to get happy again, got divorced. The other half stuck it out. Five years later they went back and interviewed those same couples. Of the couples that stayed together, the vast majority of them now reported being happy. Ironically, the vast majority of people who took the divorce route still reported being miserable.

Be patient. Some change takes time, even a long time. This is often a challenge for many women, since women seem to be disproportionately interested in changing their husbands. Men usually don't struggle with such a concept. You see, on his wedding day a man looks at his bride and overwhelmingly thinks, "I hope you never change." Many a women, on the other hand, look at their groom and think, "You're great, but you really need some help…" That is why so many men deeply resent their wives trying to change them. After all, he is not trying to change her.

The good news for women is this: All studies show that women have a dramatic impact in changing their husbands. Married men tend to be healthier, happier, make more money and even live longer than their single counterparts. So take heart, ladies; yes, you can change your husband. But you need to view him as a l-o-n-g term project. The good news is you can eventually get a man to where you want him. The bad news is, when he gets there—he usually dies from old age. It took a while.

So while change and improvement can and do happen, you must be realistic. Truth is, some things will never change. People are who God made them to be. Married a perfectionist? He will probably die a perfectionist. Married a fun person? He will probably be making smart comments and jokes on his deathbed. Married a control freak? She will most likely be barking orders as she slips into eternity, particularly because she knows this will be her last time to tell you what to do.

I always enjoy reading interviews of couples that have been married for 75 years or longer. The interviewer will often pose the question, "So, how long did it take for you to work out your differences?" Usually the couple responds, "We haven't worked them out at all! We still argue about the same stupid things we argued about 75 years ago."

I often tell couples at my conferences, "Life is hard. The truth is, what your spouse does may very well irritate you until the day you die. The good news is: You die."

Be patient.

Be
DEAD

"Whoever tries to keep their life will lose it, and whoever loses their life will preserve it" —Luke 17:33

BE DEAD

"Whoever tries to keep their life will lose it, and whoever loses their life will preserve it" (Luke 17:33).

I T IS VIRTUALLY IMPOSSIBLE TO READ THE NEW TESTAMENT AND NOT COME AWAY WITH THE OVERWHELMING SENSE THAT GOD WANTS TO KILL YOU. Oh, not the physical you (put down that knife), but the *selfish* part of you.

"Whoever does not take up their cross and follow me is not worthy of me" (Matthew 10:38).

"Whoever tries to keep their life will lose it, and whoever loses their life will preserve it" (Luke 17:33).

"Greater love has no one than this: to lay down one's life for one's friends" (John 15:13).

"For we know that our old self was crucified with him so that the body ruled by sin might be done away with, that we should no longer be slaves to sin" (Romans 6:6).

"I have been crucified with Christ and I no longer live, but Christ lives in me" (Galatians 2:20).

The call to follow Christ is a call to death, to lay down our lives, die to our selfish nature, and deny our selves. This is rarely preached from pulpits today. In fact, I dare say that we have corrupted the message of Christ and taught precisely the opposite. People have been told that, "God wants you to be happy." They hear from preachers that, "If you have enough faith, you can get anything you want." They are taught, "You must simply claim the desires of your heart." (Never mind if those desires are rooted in sinful selfishness.)

And while living a life of faith *will* result in you receiving good things from God, do not deceive yourself: God is not waiting in heaven for the first opportunity to give you everything your selfish little heart craves. Nothing could be farther from the truth of the Christian message. God wants to kill the selfish part of you—not bless it. And there is no more perfect institution designed to kill you…than marriage! You cannot stay selfish and stay married. Eventually, one or the other has to give. And make no mistake, all marriages that end do so for only one reason: One or both get selfish.

Here's a radical concept: What if God has no interest in turning your marriage into something where you can get everything you want? What if God *wants* your marriage to be in a place where your immediate desires are frustrated by your spouse? What if, instead of hearing you ask, "Oh God, change my mate," he would rather hear you say, "Oh God, help me to die to my selfishness"?

Do you know why the Bible teaches us to die to ourselves? Dead people are easy to get along with. They really are. You can ignore them all day and they never get upset. You can poke them with a stick and they never hit you back. They never complain if you fail to meet their emotional needs (mostly due to the fact that most of their needs are pretty low). If you don't clean the house in a perfect way (hiding stuff under the couch or stuffing what is on the counter into the contents of a single shelf), they don't care. You won't hear a single criticism from them. Dead people are very easy to get along with.

Jesus gave us this parable:

"Very truly I tell you, unless a kernel of wheat falls to the ground and dies, it remains only a single seed. But if it dies, it produces many seeds" (John 12:24).

Boy, if that doesn't describe a lot of people. Stuck in the ground, refusing to die to themselves, upset that they are alone, cold, unable to move, can't see anything and are breathing in dirt. Then they go in for counseling…

"What can I do pastor?!"

Here's what you can do: DIE ALREADY!! Because if you will learn to let go and let God, you will burst out of that dirt into the sunshine of his glorious grace!

Be dead.

ABOUT THE AUTHOR

MARK GUNGOR is one of the most sought-after international speakers on marriage and family and is the creator of the Laugh Your Way to a Better Marriage® seminars. He is the CEO of Laugh Your Way America! and pastor of Celebration Church. Married for 40 years, Mark and his wife Debbie have two married children and six grandchildren. Learn more about Mark and his ministry at www.markgungor.com.

Notes

Notes